BOHUSLAV MARTINŮ

First Sonata

for

Flute and Piano

Associated Music Publishers, Inc.

DISTRIBUTED BY

HAL•LEONARD®
CORPORATION
7777 W. BLUEMOUND RD. P.O. BOX 13819 MILWAUKEE, WI 53213

To Georges Laurent

FIRST SONATA

I

BOHUSLAV MARTINU

4

II

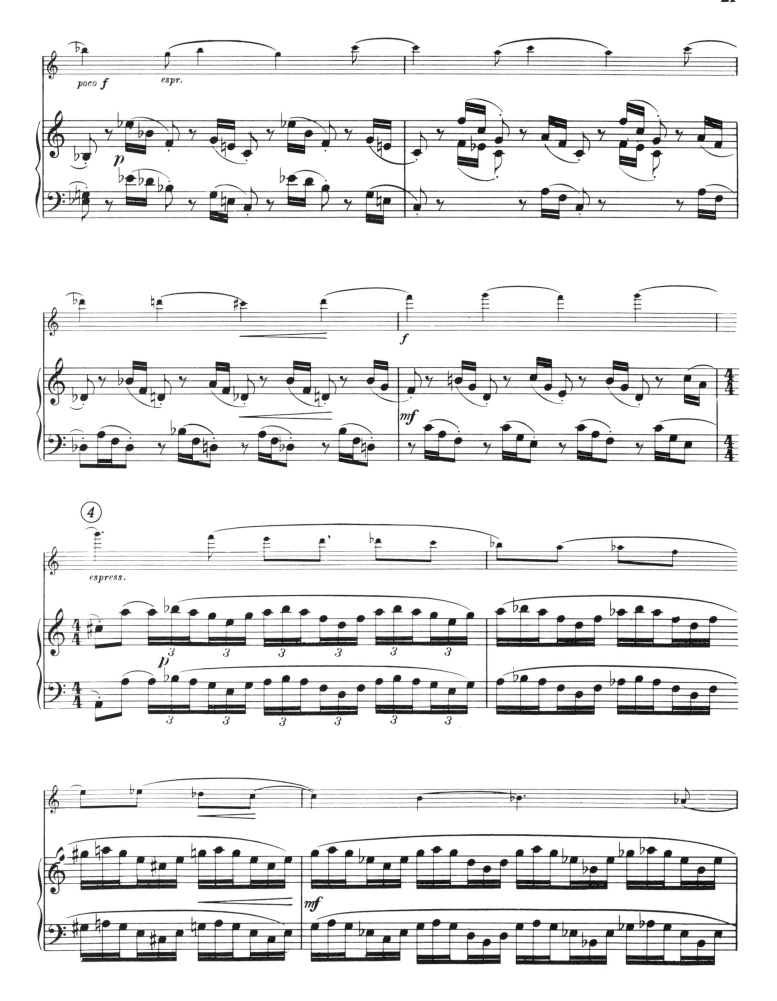

III

33